Early Praise for *Good Housekeeping*

"Whitacre's *Good Housekeeping* is a piercing gaze into the locus of human life, the home — or "this cave, this tree, // this realm where loved ones circle and unwind." Whitacre takes on timeless themes and in a contemporary context, touching on consumerism, war, and the climate crisis, while also entering an intimate space where mundane domestic scenes connect to what makes us most human: love, memory, and grief."

— BOOKLIFE REVIEWS

Praise for Whitacre's debut collection, *The Elk in the Glade The World of Pioneer and Painter Jennie Hicks*

"Side by side with the paintings, Whitacre's book serves as a deeply personal yet relatable account of one woman's life and turn-of-the-century lifestyle — and clearly demonstrates why this talented painter and pioneer stands as someone to remember."— BOOKLIFE REVIEWS

"A lovely and delightful read that brings the America of pioneers and homesteaders alive."

— CHARLES RAMMELKAMP, *COMPULSIVE READER*

"Bruce E. Whitacre's ability to capture this support network and the extraordinary efforts of Jennie Hicks in a manner that reaches beyond the usual literary or arts reader makes her story appealing to a much wider audience."

— DIANE DONOVAN, *THE MIDWEST BOOK REVIEW*

"Whitacre ends his book with an encouraging image of relationships and shared memories, and I wonder if this is why so many of us find family history so enthralling. Our links to the past can tell us everything about what we ourselves will eventually leave behind."

— Benjamin Schmitt, *At the Inkwell*

Good Housekeeping

Also by Bruce E. Whitacre

The Elk in the Glade: The World of Pioneer and Painter Jennie Hicks
Forest Hills, Queens: Crown Rock Media, 2022

Good
Housekeeping

Bruce E. Whitacre

POETS WEAR PRADA • Hoboken, New Jersey

Good Housekeeping

Poets Wear Prada
533 Bloomfield Street, Second Floor
Hoboken, New Jersey 07030
http://pwpbooks.blogspot.com

First North American Publication 2024
First Mass Market Paperback Edition 2024

Grateful acknowledgment is made to the following publications where some of these poems have previously appeared:

The American Journal of Poetry; *Cagibi*; *Dear Booze*; Epicenter-NYC.com; *GAS*; *Hey, I'm Alive Magazine*; *Impossible Archetype*; *Life and Legends*; *The Mandarin*; *Nine Cloud Journal*; *North of Oxford*; *RFD*; *SLAB*; and *World Literature Today*.

ISBN-13: 978-1-946116-27-7   ISBN-10: 1-946116-27-0

Library of Congress Control Number: 2023940554

Publisher's Cataloging-in-Publication data:
Names: Whitacre, Bruce E., author.
Title: Good Housekeeping / Bruce E. Whitacre.
Description: Hoboken, NJ: Poets Wear Prada, 2024.
Identifiers: LCCN: 2023940554 | ISBN: 978-1-946116-27-7 (paperback)
Subjects: LCSH Whitacre, Bruce E. | American poetry—21st century. | Marriage—
    Poetry. | Biographical poetry. | BISAC POETRY / American / General |
    POETRY / LGBTQ+ | BIOGRAPHY & AUTOBIOGRAPHY / Memoirs
Classification: LCC PS3623.H5624 .G66 2024 | DDC 811.6dc23

Printed in the U.S.A.

Front Cover Image: Roxanne Hoffman
Author Photo: Federico Pestilli

For Pierce

Are we where we live, or are we what we think?
Which matters? Stones or ideas? Stones or ideas?

— DAVID HARE, *VIA DOLOROSA*

Table of Contents

Good Housekeeping

Good Housekeeping

I sing the body domestic in sonnets Hooveric
The hausfrau on the corner is heartless to my dog
But her pressed curtains part on a promise of paradise
Without home fires there would be neither war nor peace
It left the boot print of settlers on stolen lands
Of those they called *savage*. Housekeeping is why
Greed is the root of evil yet it keeps us alive
Bow of that Mayfair Amazon, Mrs. Dalloway
A feather duster is our sword of Damocles
Dismiss its implications at your peril
Our polished windows gaze out unobscured
On the dwindling Anthropocene vista
The clear-cut wastes we've washed down the disposal
It can't go on like this; this is all we have.

Dinner is Served

Apples only somewhat beguile
Damask dreams a table set for dinner into being
Everything is domestical
Evening shadows reflected in the mirror
Sigh singly down the wall
Making darkness for the candles
The guests arrive
Serving salamander flambé to inspire survival
I want to etch the contours of that lean torso
Passing asparagus with my mouth but will
Save it for dessert
The paralysis of regretting an entire moment all night
A crushed pillow could mean anything
A dose of silly here lances a broken heart there
The dog asleep under the table is the soul's repose
Fondant is as much fun to say as to eat
Dinner parties always end in suds and scraping
The night of, or, if you're lucky, the morning after
The candles gutter and the gathered faces crack before melting
Into the realm of streetlights, stealth and miracles

Station Square

I will walk to Station Square
Though I won't take the train
or check out new cocktails at the bar.
I won't worry about departures or arrivals,
weather delays or locked waiting rooms.
I haven't looked at a schedule for weeks.
Tickets crumple in my pocket.
The trackside trees are leafing out without me.
The funny man who pees all the time
is no longer a comfort station customer.
The pushy lady who grabs the first seat
must now roll easily from kitchen chair to couch,
I suppose.

We gaze at screens, not out the windows
of the empty trains passing by without us
Through a region frozen in emergency,
of seething hospitals and blinded shops.
Trains clack over the heads of parents juggling children
and accounts unaided and without success:
too much out of reach; too much passed them by;
too many cash-earners gone.
Their losses will pull the spikes from all our rails,
knock the train from the trestle,
and there will be nothing to wait for
coming round the bend.

I turn back down the silent streets
and walk home from Station Square.

02/20/2022

Matching all the sox
Folding, smoothing the wrinkles
Life is a laundry bag.

Toshiko's Cup

The smaller the bowl,
The more precious the tea.
Or is that just a rumor,
An echo from Rikyu's suicide?
The exquisite dissolves in the mundane,
leaving the residue of this wave-washed vessel:
A paradox,
Solved only by use.

Rainbow void in clay,
Fired to hold rare infusions,
Sipped by refined lips.

More Berry than Brine

Holidays in marriage:
Some years the nice times kick in early
but don't always stay.
Maybe a longer glance,
words more berry than brine
before the door slam
the silence
broken by a sigh

Why do such treacherous shoals skirt special days,
their false treasures nested with dream dragons?

Maybe you've given up expectations ages ago.
But there's always a live cinder to fan,
the wrong word at the wrong time
the good walk ruined.
These confounded days
To do nothing is to surrender

Maybe you're still speaking by lights-out.
You squeeze the hand under the pillow
that will be there next year.
The snore is a soothe
And the next day back to a quotidian simmer

Maybe heat is life.
Maybe the effort is the success.

Hunting and Gathering

Hunter-gatherer reenters the fire circle
unshoulders the day's, the week's provender,
home from the market.
Genetic echoes from pre-tribal times — pack times —
expressed by car keys returned to the proper shelf.
Fridge restocked with today's deal on frozen mastodon
the hunter's only wound an ego-bruise at checkout
cut off in line by a mink in sneakers
salved now by a bargain Malbec in a juice glass.

With you these sapiens rituals ascend
to a fantasy fulfilled — two men
folding from the same laundry basket
decades of prints sepia on the shelf.
Only dim margins unshared:
childhood . . .
a stray night on an isle long ago . . .
regrets and resentments simmer beneath
in a savory stew of day-to-day
digested into weekend jaunts and wondering
where to vacation next year
or what Julia Child requires of the Hunter
to make Tuesday's *boeuf bourguignon,*

for she is the badge of the apex.
Gourmet dishes need stayers and finishers.
You gaze across a thousand tables
ten thousand tables under lights
incandescent, fluorescent, halogen, LED, and, yes, candles
that light the eyes that have seen
the Hunter stumble, the Hunter fail,

and still gaze back through the steam
knowing and yet still here, anyway.
The seer, the seen, and the savor
the fruits of the snare.

The Foldout Couch

His force thumps the entire divan
against the renter-white wall,
adding to the small dents.
These are the good years.
Galaxies revolve like the club door, powered
by magnetism and mystery.
Tossing cushions is foreplay,
though sometimes here the fizz goes flat.
A bicep in the red lava light,
an ass in the veil of blue smoke, its globes
green glitter-strewn and sweating. Heaving
planets and stars call
to the white light between the eyes,
the fire in the throat
as you take all he's got.
The collapse, the caress, the clip
of the spring through the mattress.
Another notch in the floor.
Counting down the security deposit.

Once More for Elizabeth

The proper English girl who went to Moscow in 1957,
a British Communist teen,
then you motorcycled from Spain to Rome
typewriter on your back, seeking work.
Thirty-five years later, you retired to London
after Kabul, Todi, Jakarta, New York, Khartoum, Aventino,
    Palermo.

All this loomed like ancestry behind
your terror-circled eyes when we knocked
on your door one winter's eve,
to dine out and catch up, you had said.
Yet here's a solitary dinner and a single
glass of wine on the sunroom table.
"Bar opens at 6," you say, laughingly pouring.

A roundelay of questions answered and answers lost:
Why weren't we staying upstairs? Eating in?
Again and again the same questions and answers.
Your twilight gradually dawned.

Finally convinced to dine out
you go upstairs to change.
A while later, to our relief, you return
wearing the same sorry top and slacks.
Still, oven off, and so are we.
You almost remember our names.
We eat Italian, a shared lore,
yet you mention nothing from before,
only nod and agree as we remind.
To my shame, we let you get the tab.

You nearly wept as you pleaded
until I realized that for you now,
to buy us dinner proves you remember us.

Promenading in the treetops at Kew,
mocking Fortnum & Mason at Christmas,
then catching you there the next day,
lunching at your club on Green Park,
Pompeii at the Museum,
Sam Shepard onstage in New York,
inspecting your Umbrian gardens,
driving from Heathrow to breakfast with Kitty,
fireworks over Central Park on New Year's Eve,
jet-lagged dawn breaking gray in your garden,
now I remember for you.

You say your car is in the garage
just as we pass it on the drive.
Who is watching over you and all the risks,
such as strangers like us conning a meal?
Open letters from months ago sit on the counter
as aide-mémoire, a medicinal booklet.
All is reasonably clean.
Ah, dear friend, they are calling
and you hear them.

We promise to see you again soon
as you shut and double-lock your door.
For now, this jar is full.
For love you as we do,
distance divides us.
And our memories, even this one,
spill into the void.

04/06/2022

A lover of birds
The day Dad died how they flocked
Thirteen years ago.

Nightingale on East 19th

At dusk the purple shadows spill out
around the gingko tree skirts.
Yellow-violet streetlights ignite
after-work smokers on stoops.

The corner bar casts a blue glow from
some game broadcast from somewhere
Across the street the deli flowers beam
red, yellow, and pink little fires.

Standing still with my bag at a light,
I silence the jostle of pears and ginger ale.
Stray meadow tracks pierce my ear:
the notes of an improbable nightingale.

Transmuting twilight into sound
chanting the promise and loss of night
silence aches with each caesura
then singing again, arcs of awe.

A heedless siren squelches the spell, then
you flutter in the fan-leafed trees.
Again you ignite the air in sound,
sanctify this hectic honest hour.

War&Peace@Target

Walk past the warning signs and guards at the door
into the benevolent departments of lifestyle cures:

Songbirds   fall to the earth

hungry, thirsty, naked, unsheltered, unwell, unfree, unburied
whatever the corporeal gap
the plug
is only a scan away.
SKU by you don't know who.

The dispossessed   take the streets

No matter that your shopping basket also bears
the weight of the gloved hand of the stocker,
of the last breath of the trucker.

Seawater   laps doorways

The shelves carry more than solutions.
The hornet buzz of headlines swarms the blood-red lanes.

Drones   blade skies

All for the hunt, the list and the labels;
if it can't be charged it can't exist.

A father   faints in the hold

The reptile brain is as far as Target can take you:
snake coiled but deaf and almost blind,

jaws endless, stomach bottomless.

A child   wanders desert bureaucracies

Peace has turned into some kind of war,
a war that you taste in the very air of the store.
Denial persists: there are no warning signs,
no guards at Target's doors, no,
the focused shopper lines up and checks out as before,
items bagged like the trophies they are.

Families   empty pantries

Sorted

There. Don't put this on top of this.
This is not for those to be put like that.
Here is for those that go there.
That is where you should put these.
Here is for things that don't belong there.
There is nothing like these here.
Here is where nothing should be put like that.
Those things stay over there.
This shouldn't go there like that.
That's why those things stay over here.
These things like that go here.
That there belongs with those, not these.
Those should not go there on top of this.
There, there, those go here like these there.

Mother's Chair

Another day in the arms of Mother's chair.
Her legs have been repaired and
she wears a new damask dress.
Her lap warms to cradle my yawns
as I lean back and rest my head on hers.
I wake and several seconds have passed,
maybe five thousand.
The sun has sunk a full notch or more.
Shadows of tree branches lace the walls.
The bell tolls a longer hour.
Soon the ice will rattle again for the bourbon,
the pouring, shaking, downing, rinsing.
Then another nap in Mother's embrace
or a binge-watch forgotten by midnight,
slipping off to dream
of the battles dodged and the loves unsought
of the antimacassars of the mind
of the blades sewn into the upholstery
to wake again and find Mother
beckoning in the sunbeams of morning.
Another day in the arms of Mother's chair.

12/31/2020

Raining drumming the roof
Snare stuck in farewell tempo
A year in retreat.

Narcissi, We Drown in Our Own Eyes

I love you like a leisurely country drive, the curves, the gradients.
Coffee steams the windshield. We lean into the radiance.

We were gangly colts, our love on first feet.
Remember how we teetered toward radiance?

My shoreline dissolved into yours, a safe blue harbor
the years of tides and breezes polished our beaches to radiance.

I love you like a contract I negotiated with myself.
You are my clauses, my deal, my counterparty radiant.

I love sliding under your chassis to see how you're made.
Your grime anoints my lips with its radiance.

I love you like an old oven crusty with drippings
of the problems we braised, oozing with radiance.

As the checkered flag waves around the bend
I love your hand on my shift in this radiance.

After forty years, I am your Bruce, setting another table,
breaking bread and feasting on our radiance.

Loading the Dishwasher

The phrase itself evokes a certain privilege.
I've lived with and without and with is almost better enough.
The casserole, the sushi board,
the tagine, the wok —
never Grandma's china —
it all goes in. More merry.
Slosh slosh and a gentle ping; lift and fling;
flight to the shelves that hold
all you can handle sometimes.

Some days it is the only door that opens
to you or that closes on your mess.
"I'll handle this." Click.
Words of a saint.
Heavy Duty. Light China. Normal Wash. ProScrub
To Heat Dry or not is the only
decision I am up to today.
Opinion is divided over how green is my vice.
One more dilemma to rack and stack.

Even so there are times dishes tower in the sink,
a wine glass shatters, shards nestle in the silverware,
a spoon lurks near the drain unreachable.
Those days are the days . . .
You want to load your job, your mate, your boss,
your bills, your kids, those walkers, that customer,
the news, Washington Beijing Brussels Palm Beach
your mother, your body, your anger, your hunger
your fears for the future, locked and loaded —
Cancel/Drain.

Midsummer Midlife

Come pillow against me and let's savor a Netflix.
The bed is stripped to sheets; the A/C catches up.
A sexy show and your weight on my chest launch
Beta video memories that have outlived their player:
fuzzy snatches of escapades, glances
across fog-filled rooms lit by smoldering
flickers of "bring it on" halo your face lit by the screen;
that detonate under my skin this Saturday night
that descends from velvet ropes, then chains, then spiked
collars, the bind that ties, confines — that couch.
Now we leave parties early or blow them off;
we turn away from other greener mouths
back to now — yes — scan the menu.
This is still the one recommended for you.

08/20/2020

White petunias
Banked on neighbor's patio
Bright invitation.

Witnessing Rome

Oleander on the balcony,
odor of Cif in the tiles,
the possessive calm of the *casalinga*
dusting marble sills,
puffing her Chesterfields.

Witnessing Rome,
its clichés defy reinvention.
Every fountain, every day
is both new and eternal,
documented and undiscovered.

Background,
Foreground,
the lens toggles
a rumble of tires on black cobblestones.
squadrons of scooters surf streetcar rails.
Internet marketers sip Illy
and rest their mobile phones on marble scavenged from —
why not? — Cicero's atrium.
Their pipe leg trousers bunch on soccer calves.
Their eyewear sets trends.

The black Mercedes growl the narrow lanes.
The *onorevoli* stroll arm in arm to lunch.
They plot obstruction by the fountain
under tan umbrellas
while Easter pilgrims follow their shepherds' umbrellas
from dome to dome,
gelato to pizza to *pensione*.
They pause in the same piazza,

Yet tourist and functionary never connect.
Two ghostly planes
ever parallel
hear the same splash
and move on to the same different days.

Witnessing Rome,
suspended between epochs,
seeking apotheosis in ceilings.

Night Writer

August. I am sleepless and stuck in Rome,
working a job from someone else's dream.
Tossing off clinging sheets I go to the window
and widen the shutters for more air.
Faint stars sprinkle the golden dome of Roman night,
its fetid haze of hiatus.
Their lights are almost audible in the vacated silence
of cats hunting the ruins, of the red-lamped naves.
The sweet mountain zephyr —
and only on this sea does "zephyr" pertain —
descends from the hills,
flushes the day's dry heat out to sea and
soothes my beaded brow.

A rat-a-tat-tat catches my drowsy ear:
a drumbeat, then a cymbal — someone is typing.
From my aerie the stories of windows
wrap around the courtyard in a 1930's grid.
Geometry was progress then.
One or two lit windows sentinel the shadows.
The erratic rhythm almost echoes, traceless.
It is a sound soon to be silenced for all time,
that tap-tap-tap-ching of the 20th-century lyre.

It calls to my storyteller, my bard, my troubadour.
I listen and yearn to take a seat,
to crank a slice of paper and carve with those keys
a lament, a tirade, an epic launched
by a golden apple, a lullaby . . .
or how it feels to gaze out on an August night and hear
someone's mind at play, inviting me along
to leap from this life and incise a new story.

Sunday Morning

Sunday morning on the parquet
Sunday morning on horseback

Sunday morning picking lice from her hair
        ... with a rosary and prie-dieu

Sunday morning with eggs Benedict
    ... hiking the trail

Sunday morning loading the llamas to flee
Sunday morning taking down the bodies hanged as warnings
        ... lining up for rice and clean water

Sunday morning in the dog park
    ... digging someone this trench

              ... flying home from the slopes
Sunday morning throwing that fairy from the roof
... dodging a drone

Sunday morning building Legos for the little guy
    ... cruising garage sales for Depression glass

Sunday morning spraying down the roof
    ... probing for eels in the Keys

Sunday morning pulling corpses from the fence
    ... teaching the porter how to read

Sunday morning reviving the witness for more

Sunday morning God's day of rest
Sunday morning like all the rest.

Chorus of Elixirs

Gin whistles.
Whiskey moans.
Wine sighs.
Tequila squeaks.
Vodka rings.
Champagne chirps.
Brandy lullabies.
Spirits who so generously vocalize
Rim to lip to ear,
Yet I never hear from beer.

The Light as Darkness Falls

The furniture recedes with day,
as violet shadows loom from corners,
lunging across the floor and drifting up the walls,
then sinking into the chairs or reclining across the couch,
until only a lamp can clear space.

Yet how amiable the gloom when alone.
A soft cloak nuzzles eyes,
stills picking hands, and ties the tongue
into dropping ceaseless questions
and acknowledging how unspeakable, untouchable, unseeable
it really is.

Or how an artificial light
casts a delusional glow
and washes out the miracle that lies
not upon, beneath, or above, but within,
reducing seer, seen, and sensation
to one.

07/26/2020

Fireflies to shadows
Beacon the pathway to home
Neighborhood at dusk.

Aubade for My Protectors

Angels, spirits, gods of place and power
Your work begins at the dawning hour.

Your breath stirs my dreams
and sometimes whispers auguries in my ear
which I forget now as
I open my eyes to the first gray light.

In these last moments of the watch, I remember
the asthma times, lungs in flood.
Whose kiss saw me through those nights?

Who slid me down across the seat of the rolling car
as the bridge girder
shattered the steering wheel?

Who guided the little boy safely
along the ledge that day in the park when I
was the only adult close enough
to have saved him from a fall
and me from blame?

I gaze into the mirror at my face
sculpted clean of sun spots.
I decant my pills, the spells that protract my days.
Who or what steered the hands whose makings
rattle out of bottles, keep the heart on track?

Something watches over me. Someone is there.
Whoever you are — angels, totems, dharmapalas —
every day we see the axes

fall on those whom you abandon:
the hit and run,
the stray bullet,
the fatal coronary.
Bad luck, or payback?
Scoffers say it's the casino of cause and effect.
Yet every winner is superstitious.

In a parallel universe without you
I slouch, face bulbous with tumors,
immobilized by wheezing.
One eye was gouged out by that girder
I languish in jail over that boy's fatal fall.
My sick heart will surely cut short this misery soon luckily.

Instead, sun streams in through the windows
dancing among the memorabilia.
Ancestors, angels, deities of chemistry, totems, guardians,
whoever you are in your multitudes
or Your Supreme Oneness
watch with me
the sun rise above the arching trees and stay
by my side as I walk out that door. I pray.

Life on the Half Shell

We were given straight teeth, chlorinated water, and cheap
    college.
We slept where, with whom, for as much
                as we cared,
and then moved on.

No one's children were promised more than we,
                and we took it open-mouthed,
                we, the most promising.

Houses were repainted and flipped,
yards sprinklered.

Winters in the sun
made an endless summer, even
                Up North.

We sucked oysters out of shells
until the reef was stone,
the remaining water murky.
Now we sit alone,
each on our own pole.
We dot the dirty bay,
plump mendicants pumping
our bivalves in the asphyxiating air
as the water recedes.

At the End of the Day

The wounded beast retracts
his claws and hangs his tongue
to lap the waters of the den
to lie in softness then.

Where do I bring my broken bones, cut lip, my need?
Beaten on the street — Wall Street, Main Street, Back Street —
then a cold drink and a classic flick, the cracked spine of the latest
savored in the right chair — it was all for this.

For this the commute, the clothes, the long hours,
the wins and losses to the prides of the savannas.
Life begins and ends in this cave, this tree,
this realm where loved ones circle and unwind.

This is the pod from which the seed emerges,
this soil, this shade, this sunny spot
is the best shot I've got to thrive and not
be breakfast for blue jays.

Here is the ringing phone, the screen, news from outside,
intruding fist I cannot dodge. So I choose
what I can: wallpaper, pillows, taps, mates, and say
I rule this howling world at the door I try to keep shut.

Just Be

Just be
Home is wherever I am acting out being
Or, simply, being
Home is the chair
Home is the floor
Home is wherever I sit
Whomever I sit with
The cup and the pitcher
The earth for a bed
Place of conjuring and rest
Feeding and dreaming
Silence, nonspeech, nonthought
Nonbeing
Home is my body and its architecture
My hands and their furniture
My mouth and its feeding
My head and its rest
My dreams and their play
My keeping and its tasks
My life its self
Sustained.

04/16/2021

Walkers after rain
Mourning the fallen blossoms
Faces to the sun.

Remember to Live

Morning glories, hibiscus, rose of Sharon
summer blooms that last only seconds when cut
stand for the chain
wrapping the world around the stars and back:

My joy
fleeting but continuous
like a bird's song
or the ship engine thrum
cruising the straits of Polynesia
ever present when I listen.

Even foaming volcanoes promise wider beaches.

To wake in this place
is to be a trout in a stream,
a bird on a branch,
steel tempered in forge
for the mystical epic.

Something is always coming.

Acknowledgments

The author extends his thanks to the following publications where these poems first appeared, sometimes as an earlier iteration:

The American Journal of Poetry	"Life on the Half Shell"
Cagibi	"Toshiko's Cup"
Dear Booze	"Chorus of Elixirs"
GAS	"At the End of the Day," and "Remember to Live"
Hey, I'm Alive Magazine	"War&Peace@Target"
Impossible Archetype	"Midsummer Midlife"
Life and Legends	"Night Writer"
The Mandarin	"Sorted," "Loading the Dishwasher," and "Hunting and Gathering"
Nine Cloud Journal	"Just Be"
North of Oxford	"Station Square"
RFD	"The Foldout Couch," "More Berry than Brine," and "Narcissi, We Drown in Our Own Eyes"
SLAB	"Good Housekeeping"
World Literature Today	"Sunday Morning"

"Station Square" was reprinted at Epicenter-NYC.com. "The Foldout Couch" was reprinted at *The Rainbow Project* and nominated by the editors for a 2024 Pushcart Prize. Selected haiku were drawn from the author's daily haiku Instagram posts, since November 2013. Follow him at @bwhitacre.

About the Author

Bruce E. Whitacre's self-published poetry book *The Elk in the Glade: The World of Pioneer and Painter Jennie Hicks* (Crown Rock Media, 2022), a BookLife Reviews Editor's Pick, received a Second Place Award in Contemporary Poetry from The BookFest Spring 2023. His poetry appears in *The American Journal of Poetry*; *Life and Legends*; *The Mandarin*; *Nine Cloud Journal*; Diane Lockward's third volume on craft, *The Strategic Poet*; and several anthologies including *Castles and Courtyard* and *The Wonders of Winter*, both from Southern Arizona Press; and *I Want to Be Loved by You: Poems on Marilyn Monroe* (Milk and Cake Press), among others places. His poem "Vert. Verlaine. Vérité," published by *The Rainbow Project* was nominated for Sundress Publications' 2021 Best of the Net Anthology.

Whitacre has appeared on Nebraska Public Media's *Friday Live* radio program, and ABC affiliate NTV's *The Good Life*. He has led workshops and made author visits to the The Willa Cather Center, Dawson County Historical Society, Kearney Public Library, the High Plains Museum, Barnes and Noble Lincoln, and Omaha's Bookworm. In New York, he's been interviewed on Radio Free Brooklyn's *Truth to Power* show, and read his work at the Forest Hills Public Library, the Zen Mountain Monastery Buddhist Poetry Festival in Mount Tremper, Kew and Willow Books in Kew Gardens, The Jefferson Market Library in Greenwich Village, Poets House in Downtown Manhattan, and other venues.

He holds an MFA in Dramatic Writing from NYU's Tisch School of the Arts and has completed master workshops with Jericho Brown, Alex Dimitrov, Rowan Ricardo Phillips, and Mark Wunderlich.

An arts manager for over 30 years, he helped craft award-winning theater seasons while creating and funding programs in arts education and others focusing on equity, diversity, and inclusion for major regional theaters in New York and nationally. His professional career began at the World Food Programme in Rome, Italy, during the 1980s as the organization transitioned into the independent agency that would eventually receive the Nobel Peace Prize in 2019.

Bruce is a native of Nebraska and lives in Forest Hills, Queens, with his husband.

A NOTE ON THE TYPE

This book is set in Minion Pro, an Old-Style serif typeface designed by Robert Slimbach of Adobe Systems, and released in 1990 by Linotype. Inspired by the mass-produced publications of the late Renaissance, but with a contemporary crispness and clarity not possible with the print machinery of that era, even by the best of the Renaissance typographers, this modern-day interpretation is well regarded for its classic baroque-rooted styling and its enhanced legibility. One of the five or six most widely used typefaces for trade paperback fiction published in the United States over the past several years, Minion Pro is the typeface adopted by the Smithsonian for its logo. The name Minion is derived from the traditional classification and nomenclature of typeface sizes; *minion,* the size between *brevier* and *nonpareil,* approximates a modern 7-point lettering size.

www.ingramcontent.com/pod-product-compliance
Lightning Source LLC
Chambersburg PA
CBHW031935080426
42734CB00007B/700